Taking Root

Taking Root

Elizabeth Zetlin

Seraphim Editions

The publisher gratefully acknowledges the
financial assistance of the Canada Council
for the Arts.

The Canada Council | Le Conseil des Arts
for the Arts | du Canada

Published in 2001 by
Seraphim Editions
970 Queen Street East
P.O. Box 98174
Toronto, Ontario
Canada M4M 1J0

National Library of Canada Cataloguing in Publication Data

Zetlin, Liz, 1944 –
        Taking root

Poems.
ISBN 0-9689723-0-6

        I. Title.

PS8599.E56T34 2001   C811'.54   C2001-903150-5
PR9199.3.Z48T34 2001

Editor: Allan Briesmaster
Cover and section images: Elizabeth Zetlin
Author's photo: Don Holman
Design: Perkolator {Kommunikation}

Printed and bound in Canada

for Don Holman

After a while there is no arrival and
no departure possible any more
you are where you were always going
and the shape of home is under your fingernails
the borders of yourself grown into certainty

— Al Purdy, "Transient"

Contents

Choosing a Site

Instead of a Song

As birds claim territories
with the marker of song

as wolves designate boundaries
with the scent of urine, we

score the earth
with rows and fences

move about by
triangulation, a device

known to all
animals, taking us

from subject
to object, a geometry

we find so difficult
because the third point,

desire, always
seems to be moving.

Transplant Shock

No matter how gently I dig around a plant,
cupping roots in my hands, keeping intact
the ball of earth, opening up the earth again
in just the perfect spot, returning
to the same height, best side forward,
adding compost and manure,
tamping down the soil,
watering in well, fertilizing lightly
with a high middle number,
shading from the sun —
there is a withering, a curling back,
a slight yellowing, a long hesitation.

So why am I surprised, when, forked apart
from you in the city
with only two weeks notice,
I wake at four in the morning
aching, missing the little root hairs
of my life —
                the way you respond
to "What are you up to?"
with "About five eleven."

Or riding your mustache,
the mayonnaise you claim
to save for later, as
I reach to brush it off.

From poets and books on
every corner to empty fields.

From friends an easy walk
to a two hour drive away.

Feeling this move
in every fibre.

First Day Back

Must press white jacketed cloves
index finger deep.

Preserve flavour and heat of
all kinds. Poke things down

a certain depth. Make sense
of disconnections, these weekly

leaps from concrete
to trails of fallen leaves,

from the side of brain
that measures,

that makes lists of things to do
here and in the city, that

sends me to town to return
library books, that insists

I feed on ruby chard
lightly steamed, no oil.

To the side that allows me to curl up,
a bulb tucked away from
digging claws, mulched
with thick layers of nonsense
words buzzing like cluster flies
fierce in their belly-up spin.

I wake to a dream of really
talking with my father.
He is telling me to visit the secret
place on the cliff above the river
where plump tongues of moss sprout
so soft a green you know
you must lie down,
let your eyes wander

through the pine canopy, blue
and green moving so slowly
a grouse struts by without
even a flutter
and you smell leaf becoming humus
and chickadees sing
the sounds of thunder
hawk swoop   leaf shiver
soak through your fleece jacket
as an envelope of light opens the sky
and out falls a letter
from an old friend

the day shaping up like a giant
sunflower leaning over so far
you have to hang upside down
to reach its halo, its circle
of must.

Palmer Rapids

At first I wanted mastery over white
water. I would match speed
with strength, avoid
ledges and souse holes,
slip around boulders, profit
from eddies.

You and I are standing by a river.
Its name begins with M and goes on
for three or four syllables.
      For as many days
      we have been touching
swallowing smelling dreaming
         this river that begins
with *M*, rushing
        beneath, over and through us.

Here I learn the chant:
angle   motion   tilt

     angle — it's all in the approach
     motion — then you add momentum
     tilt — and finally you lean downstream

almost simultaneously and in that order
angle   motion   tilt

(Emily Dickinson knew — go at it straight
and you're done for.)

In three days we've learned
how to get out of white water
    wait until the bow has crossed
    the eddy line and draw hard!
to use cross draws
    so you don't lose time changing hands
and back ferries
    point the stern in the direction you want to go
    and slip sideways across the river.

And the dry taste of fear
as we wait above the rapids
they've named Rifle Shoot
for the go-ahead signal
  the paddle held high,
  then dropped down.

I never would have thought
of going backwards
to get where we were going,
especially on a river.
And I had never before understood
the precision of that extra second or two
when you can choose
which side of the rock to aim for,
because you are going slower than the current
   and you know
   the way to avoid the rock
   is to head directly for it
because it is the current
     that is in charge
   and really, all we can do
   is remember where we are
   and be aware of its force,
   back up when we're going too fast
and when we get off balance
   remember not to grab the gunwales
but reach out for the river
slap its softness
brace long and low into the turn
because the success of this maneuver
depends on committing
your weight to the river,
      feeling
the river's power sensing your own
knowing both are there, growing
   trusting your partner
to do the same.

End of the Line

Everything moves
underneath the limestone cliff shaped
as much by the river as the river
is shaped by the cliff
            except our survey line
clear-cut through the bush.

Like star light recorded on film,
damselflies hover on the bark
of a chainsawed cedar.
Live cedar roots, twisted by obstacles
no longer there, hug themselves tight.
Dead limbs hang around like the same
old arguments year after year.

Ostrich ferns wave to clouds
crossing the sun as the river turns
from olive green to gold.
Two maples thicken together at chest height,
growth rings merging, with just enough space
for three white butterflies to dance
above this oblong map of the world.

We sit at the end of lines we have drawn,
grateful they have taken us back to circle
of sky, curve of tree and river,
back where things come from, even
the whine of a mosquito
searching for blood.

See how a field

See how field rises up as
suddenly as memory
becomes forest. How slope
of hill becomes lawn where
bird call blends with sound
of river, where the breeze flows
from and to, where sun
and shadow's path intersect.

See how all these reveal
what master gardeners call genius
of place, where the azure
dragon and white tiger join.
Where beauty disappoints
until imagination has room
to play with what is not.

Girl Overgrown with Wisteria

for Vita Sackville-West

Hair waved the way her mother liked it,
Vita stands latticed with ribbons,
wisteria vines twisting on hem, waist
and sleeve in their climb across her chest
to become flowering handles on each shoulder.
Someone will soon lift her up,
place her in the centre of the party, tend her
with as much care as the espaliered pear tree,
a hard pruning and a bending of limbs.

Her idea of a garden — a set of rooms
like woolen socks, prickly but warm,
a place to run through, an escape
from quarreling parents where she can dream
of her own room (no hand-me-downs)
not *with* a garden, but *within* a garden,
a castle really, with a tower tall as her father
where she will wear baggy pants, become fat
and garden hard, ignore friends
who ask if she doesn't miss shopping
in the city, not yet knowing she is becoming ill
from lead in the apple crusher.

Breakfast at nine, a walk down the lane
for the mail, then to the tower to write,
and on summer afternoons, tea with guests.
Her home becoming the most visited in the country.

She will write of her love of the land,
be questioned by biographers —
Why all those white flowers?
All those poems about gardens?
Wasn't this a selfish life?
Remembering the girl overgrown
with wisteria, she will, I like to think,

just screw on the cap of her fountain pen,
take the dogs for a long walk
and return, loosening the drawstring
on her pants, to her desk in the tower.

Humus

on the ground
of the earth
hence physically
thence morally
lowly
whence humble
as in humdrum
close to humour
adopted from the Old French *to be moist*
as with tears of laughter
succulent, juicy
akin to the Sanskrit *he sprinkles*
and perhaps the Old Irish for *urine*
so you can see it's not just
a brown or black substance
resulting from decay
but an essence that urges
us to slosh about
laughing and crying and paying homage
to all the lowly things of the earth
as in hollyhock
holstein
halibut
human

Edges

You find you need them
not just to keep the grass out
but to separate yourself from
what others want you for.
You start by finding the right tool —
a wise one who sharpens
your awareness of borders.
The times you disappeared,
obliterated by a touch taken
without a yes
or deep within a no.
Invasive words that creep into you.
The silences that grow.
You cut crisp sides to yourself.
This takes some time.
You are hard packed like the clay you garden in.
You build muscle and stamina.
You show off these new borders,
but those closest may not appreciate
the work you have done.
Your raised edges, however slight, mean
they can't get to you in the same way.
They keep trying to go right through you.
You shovel up the crumbling earth
and pull it tight around you.
You like feeling compact,
the balance you have, the clean turns
you can make, biting like skis into snow.
You can edge up to anything and remain
still and hard like a blade.
You can even back away and still be there.
You realize you don't have to be
a thin sharpened line
where two surfaces intersect.
You can be any shape you want.

Maidenhair Fern

Thin as an eyelash your black stalk
separates into two and these into two more and so on
like the branches of a family tree, until
from these fine lines whispers
a seedless, flowerless history
our bodies carry like spores.

Slightly askew, like the tilt of a geisha's fan,
your stems lean into a circle,
a blink of geologic time —
from the enclosed garden where the virgin waits
for the promise of love until death do us part,
this high walled space we all hope to enter.

At first we see only frothy green,
the bounce and sway.
Not the wind that shapes
but only a blur
spreading the way a smile begins
or the slow motion bravado of a loon
landing feet first kicking up spray.

Arms aching, I carry
this bundle of fronds
and roots heavy with humus,
to grace the table
for our son's wedding.

I think of the circle that starts with one thin strand,
and all the ways to enter this enclosure,
from filling an unmet need,
to sharing another's joy and sorrow,
or the way hope doesn't even enter
until there is reason to look for it.
And how it is within the snarl
of root that we live
as much as within love.

The leaves are down.
There is only the sound of light
falling on the ground.
Your fronds are yellow and brittle.
They crumble in my hand.

Love seems so much bigger now,
spreading as chanterelles do
underground, to become one body.
Love seems so much bigger now,
still thin as an eyelash and
so much more to lose.

What I Love Here

What I love here
are the cedars, lunging
into headlights like dragons
from pop-up books as you drive
through a river of snow. Or standing
three stories high, a family of trunks bowing
and shimmying to their neighbours
through storms.
                    And their seedlings
that spring back from your touch like sweet basil
jelly passed in a clear glass bowl from hand to hand.

What I love here are the stories
we pick up, turn over
and put on display,
stories we tell over and over
until they find their own shape, like stones
tumbled by a river,
wearing each other down
as families do, until what's left
just fits
in the hollow of your hand.

Green

Avocado   malachite   celadon   lime
the colour of minerals   poetry   and slime

asparagus   oobleck   green eggs and ham
fava bean   aquamarine   sweet-marjoram

pistachio   opal   turnip tops
emerald   cabbage   wild-hyssop.

Less yellow than wilting grass,
more blue than the sky, green
is the underlying colour of all flesh
be it brown or white, yellow or black.
Actually, you don't even need green,
just put a little blue in everything you do
along with Naples yellow
or cadmium yellow light.

Rembrandt, Michelangelo, even Chuck Close
used an undercoat of neutral green.
An earth green, not moss, not khaki, not grass,
but a muted sincere green.
They approached colour with awe and abandon,
honeydew tongues in cerulean cheeks.

Green —
the underlying tone
chromatic saxophone
the colour of vowels
the desire that fuses us
that destroys us
that sapphire of pain
deepening the pigment
of all peoples.

Living Where Weather Matters

Unknown

The unknown rises like a rash,
touches down on tip toes,
hot prickle on the back of the neck,
wordball thrown without warning
as you stand, hands by your sides.
The unknown wobbles on trick knees
afraid of the light and sleeps
with three teddy bears.
                              Careful,
or you might frighten it back
into the long dark
where your tongue turns
blue with wild berries
exploding with fear of bear.
The unknown is coated
with chocolate, swept
under the rug like dust bunnies,
hovers like a hawk's shadow
scattering the thoughts of mice.
The unknown waits like the eyeglasses
on your bedside table —
one pair for seeing far and close,
the other for middle distances.
You abandon them both
to write with bare eyes.
Marks skitter sideways, pile
on top of each other like crickets
feasting on ripened muskmelon.
If we could hold the unknown
in our hands like a baby
or a glass of milk
there would be no death,
no tomorrow, no poetry.

First Gardens

While the baby napped, I tied up the tomatoes
with old cloth diapers. Juicy as a plump

beefsteak, I leaked at his slightest cry.
I was there for the taking, open

as a field where anyone could steal
a dozen ears of peaches and cream.

My milk dried on the verge of lips
and the tomatoes never tasted sweeter

that summer when I was a new mother
and everything and nothing else.

Tongue Tied

Your fingers trace the bone
beneath my eyes, melt
across my cheek. Thoughts
scatter through the pillow
like minnows, as your tongue
takes over distracting me
from all angles.

My head
          disconnects
from the rest
of me.

What do you mean?

I don't know.

I don't want to
have to
mean
anything.

Night Garden

There's a blue-black sky over us
full of stars
and a silent white cloud.

You are the wind that steals
my breath as I race,
lungs ready to explode.

I am the cat crouching
ready to pounce
on your face. We balance

on elbows and knees.
White cloud moves
to mask blue-black sky.

You be the cloud.
I'll be the sky.
Cover me.

Living Where Weather Matters

concessions	roads, not things you have to give up
predators	anything that reduces yield. Groundhogs big as pitbulls. A shameful desire to kill.
sandbagging	part of sighting in a rifle to make sure it shoots true. You steady your arm on a bag of sand, like using an old friend to test new perceptions.
goldfinches	even yellower than yield signs
silence	wakes you at 4:00 a.m., heavy as 747's landing
water	tests pure from the well, if not from the river
air	you want to breathe, a mixture of plowed fields, a fresh cut face cord, skunk
rain	a blessing, not a curse
village	five churches, two banks, three hardware stores, two gas stations
liquor store	closed on Wednesdays
eating	whole dinners you've caught and picked yourself
warnings	to unplug things of value when you leave the house, even for a few hours, and always before you go to bed.
vistas	anywhere you stand — in a field, the garden, the village — you can see a storm roll in, the sky begin to ripple like a tin roof.
palindrome	*Glenelg,* the township where weather matters, where two rivers and all parts of yourself join together and you're the same from end to end.

Unspoken Mouths

I'm stretched out on layers of cotton and foam,
in the cabin you built which still has no name.
Relishing a small book of poems, a man's life told
through body parts, starting out with what he's never
had (the vagina), with what he's come through,
with what he's always wanted, that *unspoken mouth*
where real things are born.

And though I've always had one, wouldn't want
to do without, have lost the one I came through,
I have a place, thanks to you, where I can reach
those unspoken parts, especially that organ perched
on top of my body you've shielded with
plywood, plexiglass and two slices of sky.

Inside the Sky

Trapped inside the skylight
a hummingbird thrashes
high above you,
an irridescent body.

A hummingbird thrashes
where you cannot reach,
an irridescent body.
You fear such a small death.

Where you cannot reach
you must try to climb.
You fear such a small death
frenzied against the sky.

You must try to climb,
grasp her in your hand
frenzied against the sky
choked with feathers.

Grasp her in your hand.
Calmed by your warmth.
Choked with feathers
falling from the sky.

Calmed by your warmth,
such small bodies
falling from the sky
find their way home.

Monarchs

There is a place where people earn a living
gathering fallen butterflies,
placing them back in the trees.
Imagine the soft thud
of forty six million wings, like breath
blown over the neck of a bottle or distant thunder.
In this place where poetry replaces
gold as the standard of value,
there is no unemployment.
Villagers have discovered
how to handle metaphors
without even
damaging their wings.

Lovers' Alphabet

Once the La Cloche Mountains sang
of pickerel from turquoise
lakes to the Great Bay.

Once the La Cloche Mountains were
the hunting grounds of people
who carved bells from their rocks,

until, forbidden to make mountains
sing, they rolled off cliffs
to the bottom of the bay.

*

One day, on the top of a quartzite ridge,
picking blueberries with our sons,
you told us how the La Cloche Mountains
shivered themselves down to small hills
to be near their children.

You even brought back
a piece of rock and set it
on the mantel beside
our other rocks and bones.

And every few years we all visited
the white mountains, until we
no longer traveled as a family.

Last night your rock grew
in my dream into a volcano splitting
the house open, raining fire and ash
over the city. Scorched and aching,
I tried to escape by climbing the
whale vertebra you brought back
from Newfoundland
                    and woke
to your hand

caressing my forehead.
When I opened my eyes
you were staring across the room as if
listening to distant bells.

The pressure of your fingers
left marks on my skull,
a lovers' alphabet
no longer taught, obscure
as hieroglyphics have become.

What will our children think
of these notations
when the time comes
to scatter our ashes?
Have we told them enough
about the weight
of bone and mountain?

Listen to the Echoes

I'm on my knees, hands full of the plump, the promising. Setting each bulb in its hole becomes a prayer for the kind of growth that pours from mind to hand, unfettered, the way a fall-planted daffodil yellows into spring or a condemned person composes a "neck song." Those final truths of regret and praise, fear and longing. Evoked by thoughts of the neck losing the head, of the head filling the bucket. But I'm bound more by the drivel of head chants than the clarity a guillotine brings, more by rocks than earth. My trowel meets a boulder bigger than a watermelon and I ask myself why am I planting bulbs in a rock pile. A line flies into my head — *in the rock pile of your heart.* It rumbles around. I compare your heart to an empty field *full of rocks and weeds, crab grass and old trees. Seems I've spent years watering stones with my tears.*

This isn't *your* heart, but belongs to the man in country and western songs. The man who done her wrong. Whose kind of love we have all tried to find. And before I know it I'm trying

> *to make our love grow*
> *so every seed that I sow*
> *will take root*
> *in the rock pile of your heart.*

Strange, how living in the country changes the way words seem to go together, how after the first couple of months they start to rhyme and lose some of their syllables. I found I didn't miss them. They couldn't compare to the feel of a shovel in my hand, the slice of sod or the way a pick can move a boulder. *They say compost is the thing, leftovers and leaves make the earth sing.*

I could sit for hours watching the ruffled edges of lettuce curl. But I couldn't look at words on a page. I stopped reading. Everything. Except for the local papers. Their names referred to people and the recording of stories. *The Citizen. The Chronicle.* Not to the shape of the planet or heavenly bodies.

Suddenly, letters to the editor began to appear in verse. A woman writes an ode to the farmer

> *whose price of grain is so low*
> *it's cheaper to buy than to sow.*

Another poet doubts the merits of the county's official plan. In the next paper, a poem begins with *corny verse makes matters worse,* but poems keep coming for weeks. Still on my knees, sifting through the rock pile *I keep hearing echoes, the woes of farmers,* bent to the ground, necks waiting

The Last Black Bear of Glenelg

from a painting of the same name by Don Holman

A forest of pine or spruce or maybe
balsam fir glows in the low January sun.
You bathe in salmon shadows,
creamy speckles of light
between the trees, and
have to remind yourself
this forest is just oil on canvas,
no more real than the word *tree,*
but somehow
      if only you stand there
long enough you will dissolve
into the quality of that light,
find what you've always been seeking.

You notice the words *last* and *bear*
carved into the wooden frame
painted to look like the forest floor.
Your mind is fighting not to name
      but just to be,
not ask why or how,
but step into this painted space,
let your hair stiffen into limbs,
eyelashes turn green
and hairy sinews sprout
from the bottoms of your feet
as you let out breath you've been
holding your whole life
to feed on carbon dioxide.

          You do not
just walk in the forest, you are
one of those trees.

See — the three trees on the right side,
their trunks different from all the rest?

They are imagining what it is like
to be flesh and bone. Without any
commotion or self-doubt
       they are dissolving into you.

These trees know, and they know
you know, something in their midst
wants you, something hungry and dark
and heavy with fur.
See that charcoal patch in the middle?
Or the shape that looks like a stump?

Two cedar sticks banded black
and white enter the forest, keep
the painting from seeming
too sweet, like narcissus in a closed room, or
your own reflection on the creamy surface.
The cedar sticks bend like reeds,
keep you from falling in, draw you
closer than you can bear.

Roots

Dreaming of what's buried
of what's still to come
of where they travel in the night
of what might be passed on.
If only I can hold onto something
fleshy, the root of the matter
or beauty's dark source.
I don't know why, just that
I want to hold everything
in my hands.

Leaping in the Dark

Seeds

Spin on the wings of maples, or
      invade like
            paratroopers

spread like a cold
         from a sneeze

travel in the bowels of birds

smother like tufts of cat hair

go
      under-
ground   with squirrels

      land with a low
      frequency thud
      heard only by
      elephants

generate
         more heat than a woman

hitchhike on pantlegs and socks

explode with fire

crack open under snow

         soften

from the spit of mammals.

Sprawling

of the family Cucurbitacea, genus Lagenaria, species Siceria

1.
Perhaps the first fruit not left
to chance, tended for your ability
not to nourish but to contain.

2.
At first you are all vine, grasping
whatever is near — a piece of straw,
a bamboo pole, the inevitability of release.
As lacy petals open to luna moths
you begin to swell into the shape made
by two hands tracing the curves
of a woman into the air.

3.
You wander next door as though
invited for a beer on a hot day
and you stay for the whole summer.
Impressionable as the young of any species,
susceptible to rot as you age,
a tendency to take on the persona
of the words carved into you, you
develop a *spleen*-like gash in your neck,
torn and hollow with *ache.*
Small *joys* crumple in on themselves
and *desire* collapses from the force of yearning.

(As if words could change the shape of things
heavy as melons
light as balloons
sprawling, cherishing
stretching their tendrils
towards what's before them,
thin skinned containers of our dreams.)

4.
Called quaint, pretty-pretty, ornamental —
as though you lend beauty to our lives,
yet like poetry you suffer from neglect, fragile
container of fragile meaning, reduced
to symbol — the distance
from calabash to Tupperware.

As you transform from soft green flesh
to hard straw-coloured shell
you mold a furry black and white,
a spotted grey and orange.

Thought spoiled, gone bad,
you are often discarded
just when
you become ageless.

5.
This is what I know of you —
your lenient skin,
the way you stretch,
disheveled and sprawling,
the sound of you —
seed against skin against seed.
The weight of you in my lap.
Your sweat and scar as I draw into you,
silky neck running to swell of belly.
Fully round singer of songs
shaker of spirits
receptacle and seed
twisting from heaven to earth
until I am coiled within you.

6.
You start, like most things —
from a seed and a thought
and end
full of thought and seed.

"Have you started your seeds yet?"

displaces "Hi, how're you doing?"
You're supposed to answer "not yet,"
because nobody wants to hear
you've got the jump on them, that
your lettuce is almost salad size,
your one hundred and twenty day
southern California artichoke
has leaves longer than your fingers
and twice as fat,
and your leeks have grown so long
you've trimmed them twice.

Have you started your seeds yet?
asked in the conspiratory tone
of young boys comparing notes,
"Did you get to first base?"
and the moment of hesitation when one,
then the other, considers the truth
and whether to tell.

Have you started your seeds yet?
asked by those who have never tried,
wanting to touch the growing season
through the moisture
of their questions, the warmth
of your answer.

Have you started your seeds yet?
asked by those who want
to talk of new varieties of petunia
that sprawl thirteen metres or argue
about the best tasting tomato.

And there are those who
just want to feel the word
tomato inside their mouths,
cherish the movement of tongue
to top of palate, lips pressing
together, then rounding
and opening into its final O

Tomato
O O O
TOMATO

Beets

Last night a revelation — I don't have to plant beets.
It was that simple.
Don't get me wrong, I love beets.
But they can be demanding.

It was that simple.
I don't have to feel guilty if I don't eat the greens.
But they can be demanding.
One becomes a crowd.

I don't have to feel guilty if I don't eat the greens.
Beets bulk up like items on my list of things to do.
One becomes a crowd.
Joined at the kidneys like siamese twins

beets bulk up like items on my list of things to do
to become my symbol of liberation.
Joined at the kidneys like siamese twins,
my to-do list and I.

To become — my symbol of liberation —
the separation of
my to-do list and I.
The operation will be long and arduous.

The separation of
me from the need to do it because I can.
The operation will be long and arduous.
I'm thinning out my life,

me from the need — to do it because I can.
Last night a revelation — I don't have to plant beets.
I'm thinning out my life.
Don't get me wrong, I love beets.

Target Practice

Come on, you say, just get the feel
of it, the polished wood, the weight.

The sighting in.
The recoil.

My thumb nudges, then sinks
ten bullets into the clip,

each rounded head cool
as a nipple being tongued.

They jam, the last so tight it's
almost impossible to get in,

the way some days we have trouble
fitting into each other.

I snap the clip into the rifle,
check to see the safety's on,

that small visible "s" no bigger
than the freckles on your back.

I pull back the bolt and hear
the first round slip into the breech.

A sound as familiar as a lover's moan,
demanding as a baby's cry.

I line up the cross hairs
on the tin can, right on the

O of soup and take a deep breath,
my whole body just finger

and eye waiting for release.
I let the breath go, then squeeze,

tense for that three hundredth of
a second between trigger break

and bullet flight, but nothing
happens.
            The safety's still on.

I aim again. The O of soup.
Breathe. Release. Squeeze.

High and to the left, you say.
I adjust my stance. Aim lower.

The rifle awkward in my hands.
I empty the clip, miss each time.

Rest your cheek on the stock, you say.
I lean against warm wood, suspicious

of intimacy given only
to pillows, shoulders, the inside

of my hand on the inside of your thigh.
I embrace the gun, then grip

and slowly release as if from
a long deep kiss, surprised at

the pleasure of seeing a bullet
open up the O.

And O how scary it is that
getting the feel of it reminds me

of the first time I held a man,
not sure how much pressure to use,

how fast to go, but very soon
finding out how easy it is to

penetrate flesh
make men explode.

Lady's Slipper

Most seem unanimous
in their choice of metaphor.
The Germans say *woman's shoe,*
in Russian, *Mary's slipper.*
Venus' shoe or *shoe of the virgin* in French.
In Ojibwa, *dancing slipper,*
and to Bruce/Grey settlers,
moccasin flower or *squirrel shoe.*
   Even the Greek means
   Aphrodite's little shoe
     and I wonder,
why insist on women's feet
when the swollen flower looks
more like a purse
   or a pout.

The Greeks used to put phallic objects in women's shoes.
   I imagine slender river stones
   bay leaves
   sprigs of oregano.
The Chinese found tiny shoes erotic.
   I see a woman's foot bent
   back on itself
   toes to heel
and then I remember the shoes dangling under the "just married"
sign
   and the nursery rhyme I used to chant
   about the old woman
   who lived in a shoe.

I can feel my mother's arm tighten
around me as she reads the story
of a prince's quest for a foot
to fit his perfect glass slipper.
   I know many women
   who tried to wear that shoe.

Only the Ojibwa and the early settlers
seemed to have a meaning
I want to believe in —
            the importance of dancing
            the comfort of squirrels.

Orchids

She watches him open
the cardboard box,   lift
the cool orchid as though
it were a live bird he fastens
to her satin shoulder.
The shaking pin
enters her just deep enough
to raise a drop of blood that
he introduces
to her bottom lip, offering
the sweet taste
of herself.

She doesn't know the word *catellya* or
that orchids were named after
orchis: Greek for testicles,
their roots
a rounded handful
she has yet to grasp.   Or that
the Romans believed they rose
from semen spilled by satyrs copulating
in the forest.

When she points her toes,
he slips
her high heels on.
When she bends her head,
he fastens the clasp on the pearls
her father gave her.
Where will this beauty take her?

… to the Black Angus Restaurant where bacon wraps fillets
and Shirley Temple parasols unfurl. To his parents' house where
the chihuahua eats green peas from her plate.

Damp spots spread on the front of his wool slacks.
Much later, she pulls back his sheets and discovers blue
ball-point scribbles of another woman's prose.

Marries, has a child,
divorces, remarries, buys
orchids of her own.

Now aroused as much
by etymologies as the catellya once cupped
in a young man's palm.
She has to search for his name
among others easier to recall —
phalaenopsis

miltonia
paphiopedilum.

She has waited longer for their blooms
than it takes a child
to be born, beauty
grasping tight
as a baby's fist.

Peonies

Peonies begin
        slowly
as a poem does
tightly sheathed
not even a hint
of heartbreaking
silk and satin
then the unfurled
furious passion
after a long space
with nothing to do
but wait, ants crawling
all over you
for the sweet
sap of bloom.

Peonies last only
a few weeks
a neighbour says.
They just sit there
cluttering up the border
with their plain green.
Why would you want them?

Orgasms don't last
long either, but
I'm not going to give
them up
        and by the way,
although even poems
pass by quickly, they can
inhabit you forever.

I don't know what came over me

He was sitting next to the snow peas.
On his haunches. I was on my knees

digging new potatoes. I don't know
what came over me, except that it was

sudden and unforgiving
like the aura that precedes a migraine.

The first stone, the size of a grapefruit,
knocked him up against the chicken wire fence.

Still he didn't move.
The second stone, as big as a butternut

squash, put him on all fours,
his eyes big and brown and staring.

The third and fourth stones did the trick.
He convulsed. I felt weak in the knees.

Limp I scooped him up on the potato fork,
dumped him in the tall grasses

at the garden's edge, that boundary
between what we let grow

and what we destroy, knowing
I had crossed over, bare

handed, because I was bigger and could
because I didn't want to share

because I didn't want to stop
and figure out what came over me.

I returned to the kitchen with my basket of potatoes,
boiled and boiled them and mixed them with mayonnaise

and couldn't stop shaking until *Saturday Night*
at the Movies came on.

My Sweet Love

Each fall I separate your heads
into hundreds of white jacketed cloves.
I press you index finger deep
into cool trenches and cover you
with a blanket of straw.

You don't need me now.
Unseen, untended, alone,
you perform underground miracles —
from one as many as nine or eleven,
anchoring yourself to the earth
with thin white lines of rain
and root until suddenly one day
you are forced into green.

By mid summer you've snaked
into a field of green tipped commas
that would stiffen into exclamation points
if I let you,
                but I don't.

I cut your tops off, drape
your charms like the necks
of swans over my wrist.
My first taste of you sweating
olive oil, coating
my tongue and hair.

When you begin to age
I pull on you and you
come away from the earth
with a deep sucking sound,
like a lover withdrawing
before he softens.

Hands gloved in soft red leather
I brush away your dirt and
toss you, long as my arm,

into the wheelbarrow. Saturated
with your smell and I haven't even
sliced into you yet.

I immerse you in rain water,
your head and roots
cupped in my hand. Your neck
a handle in the other,
I scruzzle you back and forth
the way I caress my lover's beard
as I lift him to my belly, damp
whiskers tickling my palm.

How intimate we are —
palm to chin, hand to bulb
as I push back your purple-veined skin
until you lie silky, naked.
I place you carefully on top
of pleasures to come, all lined up
stiff and gleaming, heads to the sun.

You pose for me
propped inside a window,
stretched out on a bed of purple thyme,
in front of a limestone column.
I kneel before you, my sweet love,
dreaming of evenings you will spend
flavouring me, the memory of you
warm and hard in my palm.

Birch Bark

This skin, this tender jacket
tears so easily, curls back
from every touched place
every attachment
each separation
as leaf from stem
Eve from her garden
you from me.
This skin carries the same name
as an animal's cry, that short
sharp tone warning us
to keep our distance
protect our own hide.
I spiral this skin into a cone
as tall as I am, thinned
to the point of a spinning top
and wide as a two hundred
year old maple. Just to see
if I can shape such delicate tissue
make it stand alone, carved
with promises of body and growth.
I know that writing into such
a seductive surface won't
bring back the tree or us
to the garden, but somehow
I am touching both you
and the tree as I kneel
dremel in hand, smoking
words into skin
to find a new way to tell you
I have made your heart my garden.

Sigh

Break a vase, and the love that reassembles the fragments
is stronger than that love which took its symmetry for granted
when it was whole.
> — Derek Walcott, *Dissolving the Sigh of History*

Buried among femurs and knuckle bones
our sighs litter the earth,
sprout from cracks in the sidewalk
like dandelions, syringes, maple keys.
Unique as the opposable thumb,
probably older than thought,
sighs seep from us like certainty,
that odourless killer.
All that breath sodden with longing,
a weight so heavy
we should warn each other
to bend our knees.

One day I was asked if I knew
how often I sighed.
No I said, and held my breath.
I began to notice how sighs piggyback
onto words at the beginning of sentences
and inhabit the middle of paragraphs.
I even counted my sighs, measured
their depth and length, charted their frequency
as they settled down beside me
innocent as farts.

My sighs found their way into verse,
rhyming — depending on my mood —
with thigh or die. They surfaced,
carved into birch bark tepees
and the green bellies of ornamental gourds.
Suddenly they were everywhere
like pregnant women when I was.

When I asked them where they came from
they said: "We are just a release of tension.
A quick exit," they added defensively,
"a way to change your mind."

Then one of them broke down and said:
"I am the sigh that means
I can't bear it when you do that
but I'll let it pass."

Another said she was the sigh that meant:
"There you go again but if I say anything,
you won't speak for days."

And then they were all explaining:
"Can't you see we are the breath of anger?
But we're not going to tell you why.
We expect you to read our minds."

I begin the long inhale
on the way to the sigh —
the sigh that means it's all over,
the sigh that says it will never be.
But instead of breathing myself out
through the sigh, I take its skin off,
turn it inside out into the thought
it comes from, and this time
I say the sigh.

Now I know how many sighs it takes
to make an ache and how many aches
it takes to make a sigh.
I have found there are many other ways
to let the breath go —
through the pucker and parch of slightly parted lips
gently down the nose with a tickle and a shrug
squealing down the tunnel of tongue
fluttering an overhang of hair
into a silver mouthpiece or
puffing into a rectangle of holes and reeds,

but best of all that slow
raspy throat suck centering
the breath at the root of voice
collapsing the collar bone,
the ribs, out through the belly,
the forehead, into that last release
of all we will ever hold.

Wintering Over

Garden Dreams

Late fall and something
or someone cries out for my touch.
Is it the scarlet runner beans,
or maybe the late potatoes?
Or you stretched out beside me
naked in my dream?
    Four bundles of sticks sprouting from your chest
    like freshly planted rose bushes, leafless
    as dogwoods against a dream of snow.

Could it be our need to care
for each other's wilderness —
those places we've left untended
like abandoned apple trees dense
with crossed branches, their bruised
fruit giving the earth a blush, that dusty red
of everything we've ever worshipped?
    Someone has hilled up your branches
    around the base, not with leaves
    or straw but with mounds of flesh,
    yours or mine — I'm not sure.

And now the crying is closer.
I can hear you moaning.
Dreams forcing their way through you.
I pull and pull and they come away
in my hands. Your dreams.
My breasts. A voice warns of hard
frost tonight and my body covers yours.
Pruned and mulched, we lie
ready for any winter.

Palette of Winter Meals

Laced with rum and homemade eggnog
we strap on miners' lamps, shine tunnels

through the cedars. Long violet shadows
tint the snow. A cottontail caught in his own

footprints turns and swims through the drifts.
Deer tracks pierce the crust near where you

left a blue salt lick. Gnawed
trunks of pine, a few feathers

on the snow, evidence of porcupine,
angels, grouse. Beneath whispers of

northern lights, we walk back to the
compost pile. On top of the snow,

a palette of our winter meals:
egg shell white, bright lemon yellow

apple peel alizarin, the
sienna of frozen grounds.

The Colour of a Dusty Potato

for Vincent Van Gogh

For breakfast a cup of cold black
coffee, two slices of dry brown toast
and all the while, the charcoal
drawing, and this man praying
for something human to remain.

He learned from men who tunneled
deep under the earth, traced
their burnt limbs, wrapped them
in compresses soaked in olive oil,
his thumb smudging moments
of fear into their eyes.

He learned from women burdened
with fields of children, sacks
of potatoes and corn, slept
in a pile of fagots, tending the fire
within him, drawing and dreaming
for someone to come along.

Not a day without a line, he swore —
dragging, hauling, changing the shape of.
When annoyed, he rubbed his hands
as if he could not stop feeling
for the things themselves.

And in the meantime believe me,
with a handshake, Vincent ...
so he signed his letters
as he lived his life, believing
even in the colour of a dusty
potato with the skin on.

After he was gone, fortunes
were surrendered, his vision
locked away in vaults, like miners

buried so deep, there is no chance
of being unearthed.
Where are their hands,
he might have asked.
Their eyes. Their hearts.

He just wanted to give us back
the way a flock of crows suddenly
appears against the sky, the curve
of a woman bending over the earth,
some part of ourselves we have
overlooked, the dream we can't seem
to remember on waking.

How are we to know

Naked in front of the wood stove
we listen to bark freezing and turn
the pages of seed catalogues,
our mouths watering for the taste
of Pink Girls, Lemon Boys,
giant Beefeaters.
                    Carnations float
over flagstone pathways not yet laid.
Starlight peonies hold their heads up
all by themselves. A New Dawn rose
climbs the fence without a spot
of black. There are no late frosts,
no weeks without a good rain.
And like high school sweethearts,
we swear nothing will come between
us and the perfect garden.
I look over to you glistening in the heat,
and for some reason I remember my plan
to grow giant parsnips in terra cotta chimney flues,
sweet ghostly roots just in time for Thanksgiving.
How are we to know this is going to be
the year without a summer?

Flow

Caught in the silent movement of white.
Caught by the beauty of a carrot
releasing its skin — dull orange strips
falling onto stainless steel.
Caught by the sadness of young life
ebbing away. Guilty and thankful
this life is not one of my children.
Afraid and thankful that this life may last
no longer than the time it takes
for the ground to turn white.

Last night or maybe early this morning
I dream of your small body washed
in morphine, doing
its hardest work ever
in the house you grew up in.
Before I know it,
you're running from that bed
as though you could escape
your own blood and bones.

In the backyard, bounded
by train tracks and the beer store,
one wall of your house missing, waiting
for a giant hand to reach in
and pick you up from the bed.
And there you are, staring at yourself
naked on the second floor, surrounded
by rumpled cream coloured sheets.

You are watering the grass in the middle of winter,
only the water arcs golden from your finger tips
as if from a sprinkler hose
and the snow is knee deep.
Your hair, what is left of it,
the colour of ripe wheat.

Hair, sheets, arms, cheeks,
the spraying water, you, the light —
infused with the aroma of bees.

Tonight, dreading the phone call,
I take comfort from the weight
of the gourd filling my lap.
My hand guides the spinning metal point
raising shreds of skin, engraving letters
that will turn the colour of honey and hay.
My fingers cramp around the swirling *s*
of *cherish* — just another word
you will no longer be able to hear
or say or write or read or think or act upon.

A word that was given to me tonight
by your close friend, my son,
a word forged by illness and loss,
by the connections that flow among us
carried by this hard shelled container
we call language, we call the human heart.
A word that says *hold dear.*

February

one knocked unconscious battling a flood during the February thaw
one with two students killed in a crash and a father in intensive care
one with a spot on her lung, marveling at the word thoracic
one in Arizona learning the desert
one who has discovered chocolate milk has calcium
one with a shoulder dislocated on icy steps, a cold that doesn't quit
one who decides to go back to school after ten years
one who gets a cell phone and a place of his own
one who receives custody of her child, only to lose the appeal
one who faithfully visits a mother who doesn't know who she is
one who makes a tape of her own songs in a voice I cherish
one who still paints in the spare room on weekends
one who lets me read all the letters from his high school sweetheart
another whose job has disappeared
another who works three
one with whiplash and breasts turning purple and green

Until the Ground Can Be Worked

Until the ground can be worked,
despair comes as often as dreams
of next year's garden.
I am monstrous with amaryllis.
Paperwhites exude their sweetness
and hyacinths explode from thin-necked glasses.

Until the ground can be worked,
we hunger within dry rooms
for contact with the earth,
each other, ourselves,
for bare ground, emerging green,
flutter of wing, the discovery
of something long buried, forced
into bloom under the snow.

Until the ground can be worked, lovers,
envious of the ease with which
others inhabit the same bed, seize
on new combinations, anything
that will help them survive,
just as pest-ridden gardeners
turn to age-old remedies —
bush beans next to potatoes,
chives around roses.

Ruthlessly they weed out
what has always been near them,
what they know best,
what crowds them now
in their search for new companions —
the crisp snap of pod
the pungent scent of scallion.

As though life doesn't come from deep inside,
but from what you plant yourself next to.

And while marriages and countries fall apart,
I am almost ashamed to admit
to a force that can heave foundations,
a slow spread under cold ground
that has to do with the strength of love,
a love that I wish could be forked apart
like a clump of bearded iris.
Here, take a few rhizomes,
I'm thick with them.

But instead, knowing nothing
else to do, I order acts of faith —
two-year-old fruit trees, an orchard full
of Empire and Golden Russet,
Anjou and Bartlett,
Montmorency and Northern Star.

Holy Days

You make a pot of coffee.
I stoke the fire.
We watch red-breasted nuthatches
upside down belly to belly
attack the suet then suddenly
arch into the air as we do
into the ebb and flow
of this winter morning
studying seed catalogues
sweeping up wood ash.

Later I discover you kneeling
in front of the bathtub, our tobogganing tube
held underwater. *Found it* you yell
and smooth a vinyl patch over the hole.
Wait say the directions *twenty minutes before inflating.*
And in one of those lulls too short
to finish or even start most things, you open
the Field Guide I gave you for Christmas.

While you recite names of flying mammals
       hognose, eastern big-eared
       Mexican freetail, silver haired bat
I undo your belt buckle, the one
with a trout leaping out of a stream.
I pull your pants off over your socks.
You protest the cold and spread your legs.
I place your hand there to keep you warm
until I return wearing the black lacy thing
you gave me, a bit of fluff and netting.
My tobogganing costume, I say.

You smile, the smile of a baby
being fussed over, full of delight,
a smile before naming, before language,
before any other gardens existed but these,
basking in pleasure as I replace your hand.

Shifting my weight, I glide
round the corner, sail no hands
over the last rise and carry you
skidding, spraying snowy drops
all the way to the bottom.

You come to rest like
a freshly cut
chrysanthemum.

Chickadees fly between snow-clotted maples.
A nuthatch arcs around a ball of suet.

Forcing the Bloom

It is not just emergence that I crave.
Not just the tips of things, no brave
furled umbrella of snowdrop or crocus.
Not the earth's bony shoulders engraved
by the cycle of freeze and thaw.
Not the waxy joy of christmas cactus,
or the cloying of forced narcissus.
Not even the bright yellow of cancer-
daffodils budded tight, admonishing us
to be thankful for what we have still
as we unbundle them, cut off their stem
ends and place them in warm water
stiff and green, as if we need reminding
how fragile life is, each time we try
to force the bloom.

Budded Black

Budded black with crows the maples leaf out ancient with energy. Snowdrops force themselves up and tongues of wild leeks thicken. My grandfather this time of year always lights the gas oven.

Sun warms our backs the way no other heat can, sparks the rehearsal of sentence and song as neighbours gather to bring Agnes MacPhail back to life, one of those women who must be moved closer to the light like a tomato seedling on the windowsill.

Hands softening in dishwater, a young woman warms up her voice with Agnes' song —

> Born in Grey County
> where the cold winds blow
> swamps full of water
> our fields full of stone
> some call it heartbreak country
> but I call it home.

Next door a painter loads her brush with two greens and a Naples yellow, strokes Agnes a field of mown hay. Smells of oil paint and sautéing onions mix with the varnish a fiddler rubs into sugar maple, putting the finishing touch on the violin his character will play.

On stages of sticks and mud, children freed from snowsuits direct plastic warriors and goddesses as if their lives depended on it. Teenage boys load their fathers' shotguns and head to the bush.

The news came over the radio in-between the weather and the sports, all day on the hour, every hour in a familiar voice, "He died,   died suddenly   suddenly at home."

Sometime the night before, we don't know when, the playwright smoked two cigarettes (someone found the butts and later I thought about the length of time it takes a flame to ignite and a cigarette to burn). He must have thrown a line once, twice, maybe more, until it fell over the low branch of the sugar maple behind his house, and at some point, maybe in-between cigarettes, he wrote his last words.

All over the country phones start to ring, we want to know the details — the kind of wire, how many beers, what the note said, who found him, but most of all — how he could have left us, and why didn't anyone suspect.

> The painter wakes drowning in raw
> sienna dripping with Titian Red.
>
> The fiddler's bow leaps from his grasp
> and plays Agnes' jig on its own.
>
> The singer's throat closes over
> and her voice won't come out.
>
> A child wakes up screaming
> "I miss him, he died, he stuck
> a pen in his heart, then he cried."

We need all the metaphors we can get if we're going to survive.

On the altar the playwright smiles in black and white as the singer rises to turn his song for Agnes into a hymn of heartbreak and regret and the fiddler becomes

> *like a note in the wind*
> *you can never forget.*

Someone recalls how his passion could both lift you up and wear you down, his dark side heavy and huge, and of course the fierce cynical times in which artists have to live. A sister says free will is what makes us human, and as much as she has to disagree, his was a choice she must honour, and already, in just a few days and nights, can you believe it, she forgives.

An older brother remembers him best in the spring, when he arrived full of promise and when he left just the same. If this had been a script, a fellow dramaturge says, he would have called it lousy and insisted the playwright rework the end. His loss immense as our sense of betrayal, and perhaps, for those closest, a relief from walking beside him on the edge.

That evening while the sky burned from grey to emerald green, I dug three holes, filled them with compost and watered in three common lilacs. "A direct hit," the familiar voice said. "Tornadoes touched down from Shelbourne to Owen Sound ... trees sucked right out of the ground."

How random the wild wind is — one down, the rest straight. All the years it took to grow and in seconds it's gone. Leaving us behind to judge a life as the earth is being reborn, asking why so many ripen only to disappear like spring snow.

I'm looking for a place to bury what up until now only the earth can contain. Three common lilacs. Their holes dug last April 19th. One didn't survive the summer. Two still under the snow, buds packed tight with fragrance and bloom.

And again before my eyes my grandfather turns on the gas, his mustache waxed, his dark eyes glazed, placing his head in the oven, long before I was born with those eyes.

Shattered by Noon

When tulip leaves appear edged in red
slow to unfurl as thoughts held tight

by memory failing, when the whole
world vanishes beneath a late snow,

green still elusive during this
season frantic with instinct,

peonies soon to emerge red
as the head of a dog's penis

and crocus flash open an ache deep
as a baby's first smile, all yellow

joy, all full of answered prayer,
dangle of snowdrop, wisp of chive,

when overnight from trees and wires
hang transparent knives that glitter

then shatter by noon with the sound
of a life breaking up too soon,

when all we can see is shimmer
and clouds of steam rising from the fields

as we begin the daily pace of garden
bounded by sweet ruthless bird song

measuring promise and betrayal,
bud and bloom, dieback and fade.

An Angry Soup

All day you have been bringing a faint sweetness to a boil, seated on a plastic bucket at the edge of the bush, fluorescent orange toque burning the sky blue, as you and the bucket slowly sink into the snow-covered hay field, smoke curling through bare maples while at the other end of the field, in front of another fire, I move bundles of words across a small screen, both of us condensing to quick simmer and foam, so easily turned into a brittle sugary mess.

We are in the habit of spending our days apart, meeting for the evening meal, which you most often prepare. You've just set the cast iron pot on the table, lifted the lid, spooned steaming soup into my bowl, cut a slice of rosemary tomato bread and poured my favorite wine.

You look at me with that pause I love to draw out, until you can't help yourself, you have to say "Well?"

"Ummm!" I say, relishing the silky slip of labial consonants, celery, the velvet mouthfeel of shitake, broth blooming with the undertaste of portabello.

"This is an angry soup," you say. "Angry? How can a soup be angry?" "Yes, angry, because it won't get out of bed, can't bear another day of snow storms, another day without sun."

You mean anger sweats the onions? Extracts essence of carrot, tears spinach into a fistfull of bits, pouring this last long bout of winter down our throats? Until somehow we become brilliant with bleeding trees and corn snow, lucky to get the proportions just right, whether it's forty cups of sap to one of syrup, a few words along one side of a page, or nothing more than two people nestling close in the night, like amber jars cooling on the kitchen counter.

April Morning   All We Can See

grey rain
tulip buds   still only hinting red
clothes   thrown on the bedroom floor, the arm
                     of your bathrobe draped gently on my
velour pants   the empty shell of
your jeans   discarded where you stepped out of
                     them still holding the shape of your ass
your brown socks   like trout rising, lie frozen midway
                     in their curl over
a pile of shirts
my socks   reach up over the back of
the chair   their oval entrances a darker blue
                     a pair of baby birds, mouths wide open
our socks   half full of your calves, my ankles
                     have turned each other inside out
their toes   every which way

87

When Every Moment Speaks

On days arbitrary as daisy petals
torn from their centre, on days
that fluctuate from a yes to a no
within the flick of an eye,
on days when all you can do
is walk within memory,
on days such as these,
thought crosses your path
like a scattered bouquet,
only it is the end of winter
and nothing flowers
                        except
the hollow step of deer,
a bone dance of hunger.

Everywhere memories pass
through the land like ghosts.
You keep reaching out to them,
notice how time bends and melts
until everything runs
into memory's thick plunk
of sap on metal
filling you with its silver dance
until morning, another frozen layer,
while underneath, memory still runs
sweet, until nothing is visible
but the song in your throat
how it used to be
wasn't really
could have been
and tonight all is white
with a calm lasting until dawn
when every moment speaks
with its own hands.

A Natural Movement

the swell of an onion bulb, a deep breath,
the slow revelation of juniper green, moss green,
chive green, dove grey, dead leaf brown

the air thick with sound and swoop of
undulating chickadees
grackles shimmering purple to blue
and back again

corn snow parsed with fresh tracks
where deer have just crossed
a stream of snow islands
raccoon paws rest delicately within a buck's step
mice prints splatter up the hill
and ruffed grouse toes point
bravely
towards the road.

Acknowledgements

I am grateful to the Canada Council, the Banff Arts Centre and the Toronto Arts Council for their support. Thanks especially to Don McKay, who worked with me on the manuscript during the 2001 Banff Writing Studio; Olive Senior (Humber College Correspondence School for Writers) who helped select and begin editing the poems; and Allan Briesmaster, my discerning editor, who took on this book as if it were his own. And for their advice and encouragement — Pat Jasper, Merike Lugus, Donna Langevin, Jim Slominski, Colleen Flood, Mary Ellen Csamer (all members of watershedBooks); Susan Gibson, Judy Lowry, and the Banff "chooks" (rhymes with "books"): Jan Horner, Lorri Neilson Glenn, Leanne Averbach, and Jannie Edwards.

Earlier versions of some of the poems appeared in: *Line by Line* (Ekstasis Editions, 2001); *The Gourd Poems* (Canadian Poetry Association, 1999); *Portraits.Sound* (Always Press, 1996); *Ghost of Glenelg* (Always Press, 1995); *Sounding* (Ginger Press); *Spring-Fever, (W)rites of Spring 1997* (Your Scrivener Press); *like lemmings* Vol. 1, No. 1; *Carousel Magazine,* #Twelve 1998; and *Mosaic,* Vol. 2, #10.

- "Garden Dreams" received first prize in *Carousel Magazine*'s 1998 poetry contest.
- "Holy Days" received second prize in the Stephen Leacock 1998 International Poetry Competition.
- *The Gourd Poems,* many of which are reprinted here, won the Canadian Poetry Association's 1999 Shaunt Basmajian Chapbook Award.
- In "Unspoken Mouths," the small book of poems is *Selected Organs* by bpNichol.
- "Seeds" was adapted from Anna Leggatt's article "Successful Seed Starting."
- "Peonies" is for Karen Maier.
- "Edges" is for Joan McAndrew.

- "Budded Black" is in memory of Clarke Rogers. The italicized words were taken from his script in progress: *Agnes MacPhail and the Fiddler's Due.*
- "Maidenhair Fern" is for Chiah and Tracy Lanzon-Holman.
- Lines from Al Purdy's "Transient" were reproduced with the kind permission of Eurithe Purdy and Harbour Publishing. "Transient" is in *rooms for rent on the outer planets* (Harbour, 1999).
- Section Three's title, "Leaping in the Dark," refers to Henry Miller's lines from *The Wisdom of the Heart:* "All growth is a leap in the dark, a spontaneous unpremeditated act without the benefit of experience."

The Gourd Poems

Considered the first cultivated plants, perhaps as early as 40,000 years ago, ornamental gourds have an honoured place in human history. Gourds have been used in ceremony and ritual as well as for drinking vessels, bowls, bottles, floats, utensils, masks, rattles, drums, birdhouses and art. They have been found in Peruvian excavations dating back 5,000 years and in Egyptian tombs.

The idea to use randomly generated words as catalysts for poems came from performance artist Laurie Anderson, who tried to write lyrics with the 100 English words most used by the news media. She found they were mostly what she called "glue words," so she expanded her list to the 258 most used words. But she still wasn't satisfied. Neither was I. Among these words were *no*, but not *yes*, *boy* and *man* but not *woman*. These words account for 55 percent of written English. I needed my own list of words meaningful to me and those I cherish.

- "Sprawling" started with Stephanie Hutcheson's description of the gourd vines in her garden.
- "When Every Moment Speaks" was inspired by Kim Fahner's words *speaking with hands, daisy* and *memory*.
- "Flow" is in memory of Jon Vise and is dedicated to my sons Ira Zingraff and Chiah Holman, who gave me the words *flow* and *cherish*.
- "Unknown" began when Ira emailed me his list of words, including *nebulous, aroma, thumb, gurgle, cohesion* and *unknown*.
- The word *sky* ("Inside the Sky") is from Susan Gibson.
- The other *Gourd Poems* in this book are: "End of the Line," "Humus," "Green," "What I Love Here," "My Sweet Love," and "Sigh."

About the Author

Elizabeth Zetlin's previous publications include *Said the River* (Penumbra Press, 1995), *Connections* (Always Press, 1994), and *Ghost of Glenelg* (Always Press, 1995), all collaborations with visual artists. Her chapbook *The Gourd Poems* received the 1999 Canadian Poetry Association's Shaunt Basmajian Award. Her poetry has also received a Stephen Leacock Award (1998), and her first short story an honourable mention at the Eden Mills Writers' Festival.

In May 2001, CBC Radio's *Ontario Today* program broadcast the poems "My Sweet Love" and "Peonies," and hosted a "Gourd Word" contest. The winner, Tracy Shepherd, received a Zetlin poem inspired by her word, "milk," and an ornamental gourd with the winning word inscribed.

In addition to writing, Elizabeth works as a visual artist, creating installations such as ornamental gourds inscribed with images or words; hundreds of garlic cloves that mature into a word of prayer; and a life-sized birch bark cone inscribed with words of body and garden. Her current project is *The Punctuation Field*, both a manuscript and a meadow (featuring commas, parentheses, the @ symbol, a question mark, and the emoticon for irony).

Born and raised in Norfolk, Virginia, she now lives in Toronto and Traverston (near Markdale), Ontario.